A beautiful book for a beautiful friend. Emmanuel, Jesus is with you.
Love,
Donna

We Hear the Angels

ANCIENT PRAYERS FOR ADVENT

JoAnn Streeter Shade

LAYOUT AND DESIGN BY KEVIN DOBRUCK

We Hear the Angels
Ancient Prayers for Advent
JoAnn Streeter Shade

2015 Frontier Press

All rights reserved. Except for fair dealing permitted under the Copyright Act, no part of this book may be reproduced by any means without the permission of the publisher.

Scripture taken from the Holy Bible, Today's New International Version TNIV, copyright 2001, 2005 by International Bible Society, unless otherwise noted.
All rights reserved worldwide.

Scripture quotations marked (MSG) are taken from The Message.
Copyright 1993, 1994, 1995, 1996, 2000, 2001, 2002.
Used by permission of NavPress Publishing Group.

Scripture quotations marked (NIV) are taken from the Holy Bible, NEW INTERNATIONAL VERSION®, NIV®
Copyright © 1973, 1978, 1984, 2011 by Biblica, Inc.®
Used by permission. All rights reserved worldwide.

Shade, JoAnn Streeter
We Hear the Angels

November 2015

Copyright © The Salvation Army USA Western Territory

ISBN 978-0-9908776-8-4

Printed in the United States of America on recycled paper

Foreword

The Christmas season is a beautiful time for the renewal of hope. We hear the voices of children and their hopes for special Christmas presents. We can hear the voices of Bible teachers who would remind us of the birth of Jesus and God's great hope for the world.

In the Scriptures we are even able to read and listen to the voices of the prophets and others who were actually present for the birth of Jesus. Truly, the voice of our hopes become our prayers.

In this new work, entitled *We Hear the Angels*, we are supported to hear the voices of the angels who speak to us clearly about our hopes and our prayers. I'm expecting that this beautiful text will support you with your hopes and prayers this Christmas season.

Enjoy searching the riches of God in the birth of Jesus and let your prayers soar into heaven. God is waiting to hear from you.

James M. Knaggs, Commissioner
Territorial Commander
The Salvation Army Western USA

Introduction

Prayer, the songwriter tells us, is "the soul's sincere desire, uttered or unexpressed" (James Montgomery). It may be learned with the childlike, "Now I lay me down to sleep," or patterned from the prayer that Jesus taught his disciples: "Our Father, who art in heaven."

Prayer may be spontaneous or scripted, verbal or silent, corporate or privately personal. This collection of prayers has been gathered from those written throughout the centuries of church history, and are prayed from the voices of clergy and laypersons. These prayers of Advent and Christmas have been recorded so that we too might pray the words during our days of preparation for the coming of the Christ Child to our world.

Read one each day, with your morning coffee, at the lunch table, or as you prepare to rest from the work of the day. Allow the voices of the ancient believers to join yours as you draw near to God.

As far as I can determine, these prayers are found in the public domain. Unless otherwise noted, the Scripture used is from Today's New International Version of the Bible.

> May the blessings of God be with you,
> May the Christ Child light your way,
> May the Holy Spirit guide you to keep you safe each day.
>
> *An Irish Christmas Prayer (unknown)*

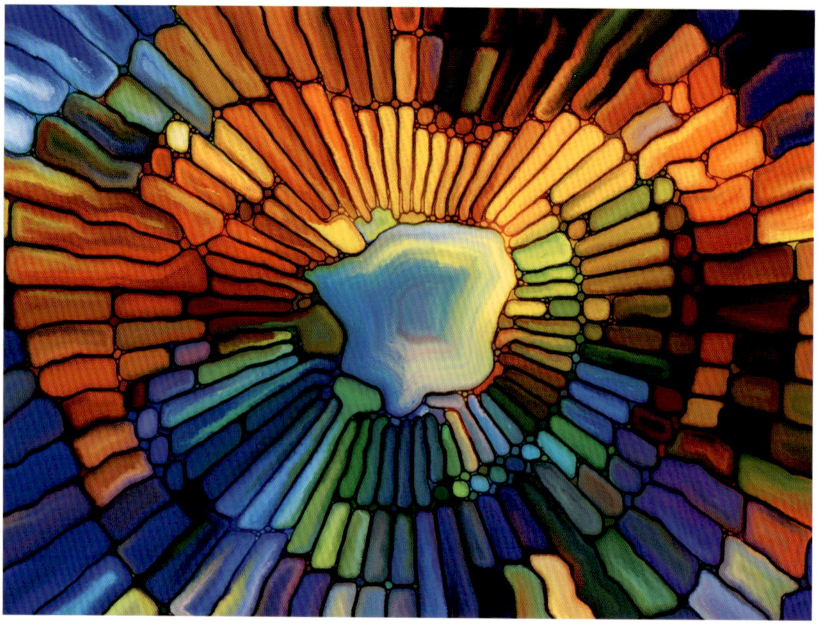

DEC 1

Nativity Prayer
St. Bernard of Clairvaux (12th century)

Let Your goodness Lord appear to us, that we
made in your image, conform ourselves to it.
In our own strength
we cannot imitate Your majesty, power, and wonder
nor is it fitting for us to try.
But Your mercy reaches from the heavens
through the clouds to the earth below.
You have come to us as a small child,
but you have brought us the greatest of all gifts,
the gift of eternal love.
Caress us with Your tiny hands,
embrace us with Your tiny arms
and pierce our hearts with Your soft, sweet cries.

The sensual images St. Bernard brings to his prayer are striking: the caress of the tiny hands of a baby, the embrace of those tiny arms, and the sound of a soft, sweet cry. While I've seen my share of plastic babes in assorted mangers, I don't often make the connection with Jesus before his adult years. When I think of him, it is as a man, striding through the crowds, sitting on the hillside, storming through the temple. Yet if Christ was the incarnation at age thirty, he was also the incarnation at the age of six months.

When our infant granddaughter strokes my cheek, I feel cherished and comforted. It is this touch, this image, that reaches me in Bernard's prayer. Ah, little Lord Jesus—in your infancy, in your manger, in your helplessness, you were God, and you reached out—in fact, you continue to reach out—to lavish your love upon us, your children. Caress, embrace, pierce—come, Lord Jesus.

Prayer Focus: the embrace of God

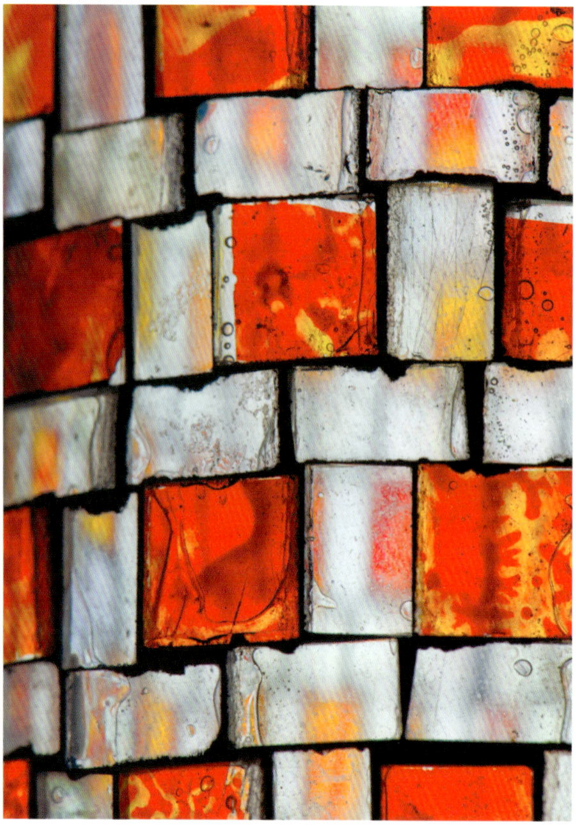

DEC 2

Nativity Prayer

St. Ephraim the Syrian (4th century)

The feast day of your birth resembles You, Lord
Because it brings joy to all humanity.
Old people and infants alike enjoy your day.
Your day is celebrated from generation to generation.
Kings and emperors may pass away,
And the festivals to commemorate them soon lapse.
But your festival will be remembered until the end of time.
Your day is a means and a pledge of peace.
At Your birth heaven and earth were reconciled,
Since you came from heaven to earth on that day
You forgave our sins and wiped away our guilt.
You gave us so many gifts on the day of your birth:
A treasure chest of spiritual medicines for the sick;
Spiritual light for the blind;
The cup of salvation for the thirsty;
The bread of life for the hungry.
In the winter when trees are bare,
You give us the most succulent spiritual fruit.
In the frost when the earth is barren,
You bring new hope to our souls.
In December when seeds are hidden in the soil,
The staff of life springs forth from the virgin womb.

Here are the true gifts of the incarnation, the gifts of the Father, through the Son, to embrace the world with a divine love (Eph. 2:4 MSG). Is your heart sick, blind, thirsty, hungry, barren? The gift of life was born in that manger for you, for me, as heaven and earth were reconciled. While Johnny may have wanted a pair of skates and Susie a dolly, God knew what the world needed: light, salvation, the bread of life, spiritual fruit, new hope. "All I have needed thy hand hath provided—great is thy faithfulness!"

Prayer Focus: the faithfulness of God

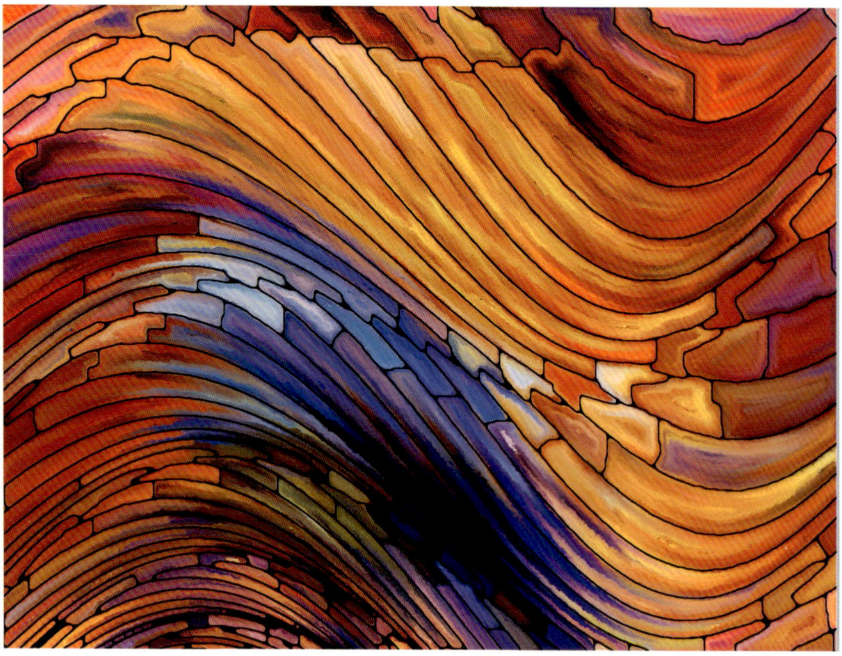

DEC 3

Christmas Prayer of Pope John XXIII

Angelo Giuseppe Roncalli (20th century)

O sweet Child of Bethlehem,
grant that we may share with all our hearts
in this profound mystery of Christmas.
Put into the hearts of men and women this peace
for which they sometimes seek so desperately
and which you alone can give to them.
Help them to know one another better,
and to live as brothers and sisters,
children of the same Father.
Reveal to them also your beauty, holiness and purity.
Awaken in their hearts
love and gratitude for your infinite goodness.
Join them all together in your love.
And give us your heavenly peace. Amen.

What prayer does a pastor pray for his/her people? Growing up in the Presbyterian tradition, each week the minister would pray the pastoral prayer, a prayer specifically for the people of the church. In the same way, Pope John XXIII demonstrates a pastor's heart as he prays this prayer.

First, for faith, that the mystery of Christmas, the incarnation, might be known to us. A prayer for personal peace follows, the peace Jesus speaks of in John 14, perfect peace, the peace that passes all understanding. And then John prays for relationships, a plea for connection, for a familial relationship as children of the same Father.

It challenges us this day to consider this: How do we—as pastors, Sunday School teachers, mothers, fathers, friends, co-workers—pray for the people in our lives? And on a personal level, what is most dear to my heart as I pray for others (and for myself)?

Prayer Focus: our prayers for others

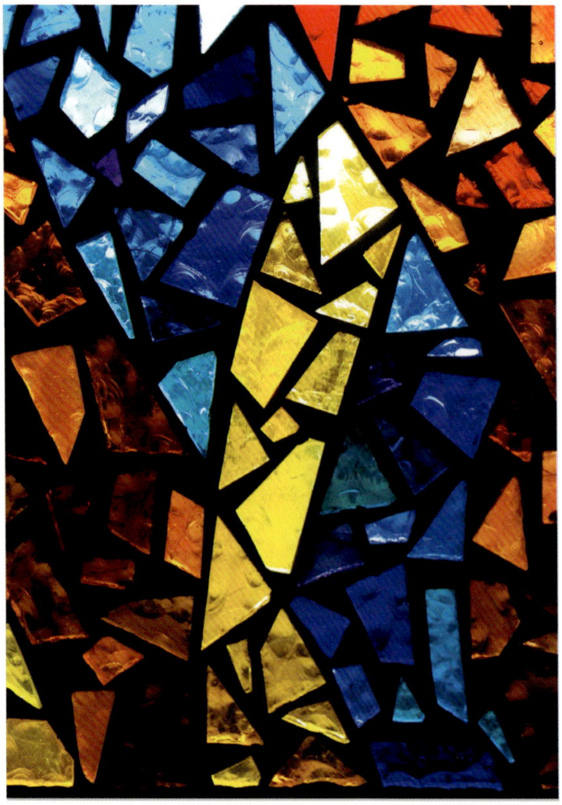

DEC 4

A Byzantine Traditional Prayer

Christ is born; give him the glory!
Christ has come down from heaven; receive him!
Christ is now on earth; exalt him!
O you earth, sing to the Lord!
O you nations, praise him in joy,
for he has been glorified!

Glory to the Father, and to the Son, and to the Holy Spirit;
as it was in the beginning, is now, and will be forever.
Amen.

This ancient prayer has the feel of a psalm, as it trumpets the birth of Christ with an exhortation to praise and song on the part of the believer. Perhaps it was a sung prayer as well, as its rhythms would suggest that a melody may have been a part of its expression.

While I don't know what notes (if any) may have accompanied its opening lines, its final line is the traditional Gloria Patri sung every Sunday of my childhood at the conclusion of the pastoral prayer. As Presbyterians, we weren't as strictly liturgical as some churches, but there was a pattern to our worship, and these words were included in that pattern.

"Glory be to the Father, and to the Son, and to the Holy Ghost." We stood in the presence of God and affirmed our belief in the Trinity, one in three, and, as Salvation Army doctrine explains, "co-equal in power and glory." Present in the beginning, at the creation of the world. Present in our day, as we walk in the Spirit, and present forever, infinitely God with us.

For this day, it will be the melody that echoes in my head.

Glory be to the Father, and to the Son, and to the Holy Ghost.
As it was in the beginning, is now and ever shall be, world without end.
Amen. Amen.

Prayer Focus: in praise of the Trinity

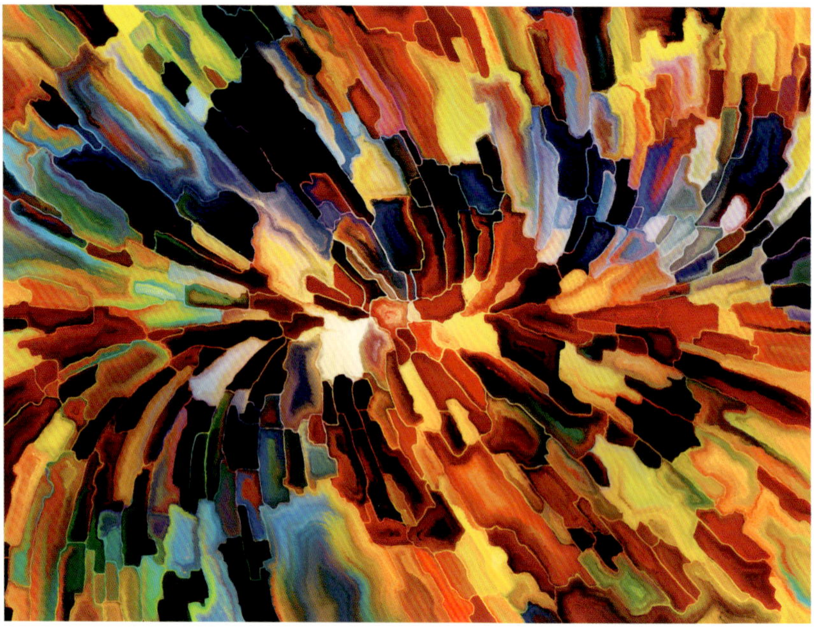

DEC 5

Holy Star

William Cullen Bryant (19th century)

O Father, may that holy Star
Grow every year more bright,
And send its glorious beams afar
To fill the world with light.

Our granddaughter, the lovely Madelyn Simone, is quite the singer. One of the first songs she learned was, "Twinkle, twinkle, little star, how I wonder what you are." Indeed, that must be the question addressed to the star that greeted the birth of Christ. What are you?

The "holy star" that Bryant writes of was preserved for the ages by Matthew, who quotes the group of wise men: "Where is the child? We saw his star in the east." The answer to their question came through the star, for *the star they had seen in the east went ahead of them until it stopped over the place where the child was* (Matt. 2:9 NIV).

Was the star supernaturally bright? Was the star at its zenith in the days following the birth of the baby? Or were the eyes of the wise men opened to what had been present all along? Perhaps the answer is all of the above.

While Bryant may have prayed for the light to grow supernaturally, it was in Christ that the everlasting light shone in the darkness. He told his followers, *"I am the light of the world"* (John 8:12). Indeed, in Him the people who walked in darkness have seen a great light.

But the light of the star and the light of his own presence wasn't enough for Jesus. He turned the tables as he so often did and told his followers, *"You are the light of the world"* (Matt. 5:14). When the light of Christ is reflected in his followers, the holy star grows brighter. "Shine, Jesus, shine!"

Prayer Focus: the light of Christ

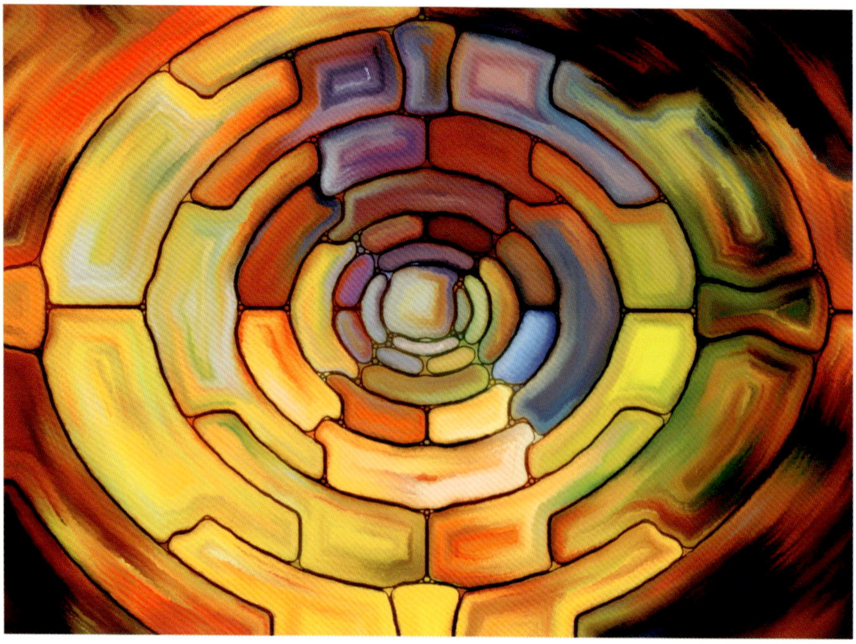

DEC 6

A Gaelic Blessing

Deep peace of the running waves to you,
Deep peace of the flowing air to you.
Deep peace of the smiling stars to you.
Deep peace of the quiet earth to you.
Deep peace of the watching shepherds to you.
Deep peace of the Son of Peace to you.

The prayer of blessing is an ancient practice, as old as the creation of the earth (see Genesis 1:28). Jesus took the children in his arms and blessed them, while the specific blessing of peace was Christ's as well, as he said farewell to his disciples in John 14: *"Peace I leave with you; my peace I give you"* (v.27).

This particular prayer of blessing is one that has been at the bottom of my e-mail for quite some time, minus the fifth line, that of the watching shepherds. I suppose I should have changed it long before now, but then I'd have to figure out how to actually change it—so it stays. Unfortunately, too many things remain in our lives because we can't figure out how to change them, but this prayer of blessing is a keeper.

Peace, deep peace, perfect peace. The theme runs through many of the Advent prayers and Christmas carols. Not, Jesus reminded us, as the world gives to us, but a peace that passes all understanding. As the running waves, as the flowing air, as the smiling stars, as the quiet earth. And yes, as the watching shepherds, those faithful ones who kept watch over their flocks by night, waiting and watching.

The images of this blessing remind us of the sense of peace we long for, but the blesser understands that the source of that peace is found only in its last line—through the Son of Peace. Might that deep peace, found only in Christ, be ours.

Prayer Focus: deep peace

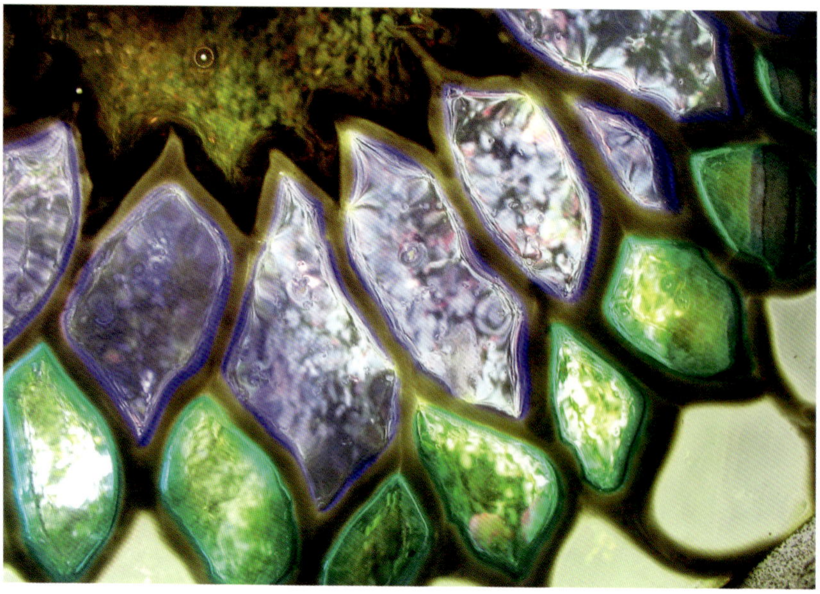

DEC 7

The Incarnation

Harry Read (21st century)

Lord Jesus Christ, you came to show
The Father's way for all to go,
That in our seeking we might find
The Father's heart—the Father's mind.

In flesh, you blended Heaven and earth,
Made sacred our most human birth;
Became God's pattern for us all;
Our means to match the Father's Call.

You came, Incarnate Christ, to be
Incarnate in unworthy me,
That in this faulty flesh of mine
Might dwell your life—the life divine.

When we contemplate the mystery of the incarnation, we most often think of it as did Charles Wesley: "Veiled in flesh the Godhead see, Hail the incarnate Deity." In the incarnation (from the Latin, "into flesh"), God became human in the person, the flesh, of Jesus. In seeking to understand what can only be fully encountered as mystery, we all too often "sweat the details" of how this could have happened, of how God's Spirit could overshadow Mary and bring life to her womb.

But Salvationist poet Harry Read helps us to ask the essential question of the incarnation: Why? Why would the God of the universe become human? While there are a number of possible answers to the question of why, such as Wesley's "born that man no more may die," the promise of the incarnation is that the incarnate Christ could then become incarnate in us. Jesus explained it this way as he spoke to his disciples on the eve of his death: *"I am in my Father, and you are in me, and I am in you"* (John 14:20).

Our prayer becomes one of astonishment, that God might even consider dwelling in our flesh. It becomes a prayer of gratitude, "that in this faulty flesh of mine might dwell your life—the life divine." And it ultimately becomes a prayer of invitation: "Come, Lord Jesus."

Prayer Focus: a seeking heart

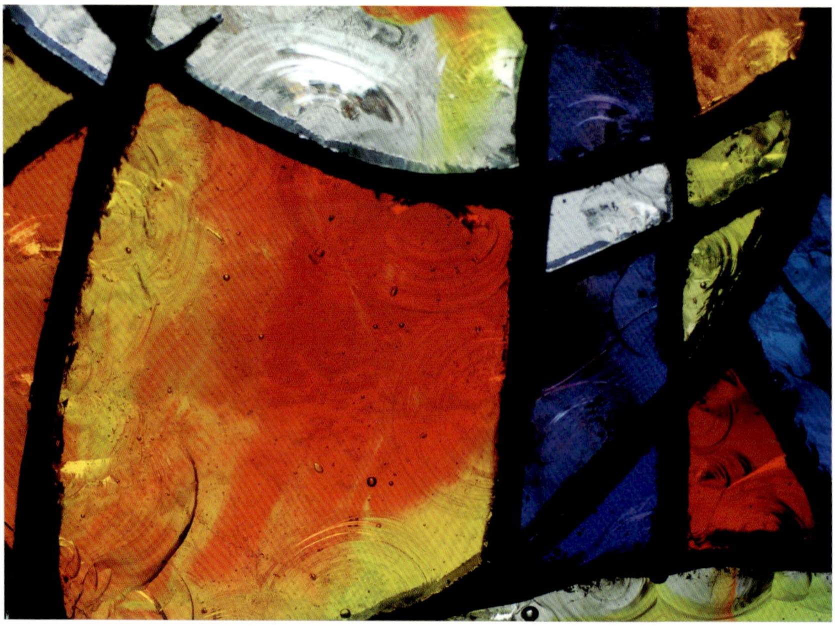

DEC 8

The Mystery of Burning Charity
St. Angela of Foligno (13th century)

O my God! make me worthy to understand something of the mystery of
the burning charity which is in You, which impelled you to effect the
sublime act of the Incarnation!
which brings to man, with the outpouring of love,
the assurance of salvation.
How ineffable is this charity!
Truly there is no greater than this, that the Word was made flesh in order to
make me like unto God!
You became nothing in order to make me something;
You clothed Yourself like the lowliest slave
to give me the garments of a King and a God!
Although You took the form of a slave,
You did not lessen Your substance, nor injure Your divinity,
but the depths of Your humility pierce my heart and make me cry out:
O incomprehensible One, made comprehensible because of me!
O uncreated One, now created!
O Thou who art inaccessible to mind and body,
become palpable to thought and touch, by a prodigy of Thy power!

St. Angela's prayer focuses on the mystery, the amazing gift of the incarnation. The Almighty God a baby. Most of us have heard the story so many times that we don't stop to think of the magnitude of that act, so Angela does it for us. At first reading, I was put off a bit by the language she used. It seemed extreme, excessive, but as I sat with her prayer, it struck me—the incarnation was extreme, it was excessive. As John reminds us (1 John 3), this was love lavished upon us.

After all, God could have been satisfied with the angel messengers, with the prophets and their attention-grabbing actions. He could have kept on with the temple sacrifices and the details of the law. But instead, immense in mercy and with an incredible love, God sent his Son. For us (Eph. 2:4 MSG).

Prayer Focus: the grace of God

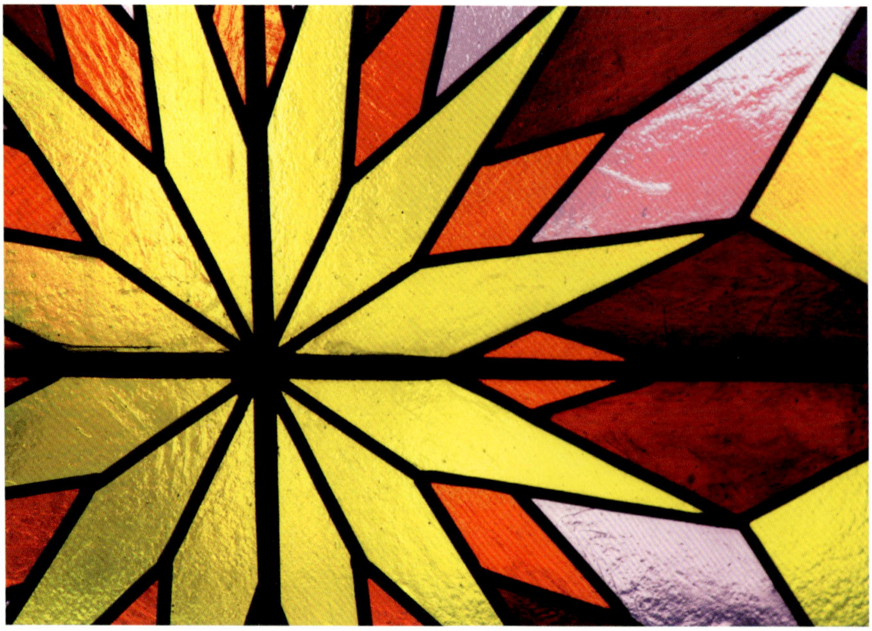

DEC 9

Morning Star (A Moravian Hymn)

Johannes Scheffler (17th century)

Morning Star, O cheering sight!
Ere Thou cam'st, how dark the night!
Jesus mine, in me shine,
Fill my heart with light divine.
Morning Star, thy glory bright
Far excels the sun's clear light,
Jesus be, constantly,
More than thousand suns to me.

When living in Philadelphia, we were privileged to journey to Bethlehem (Pennsylvania, not Judea) to attend a traditional Christmas observance known as the Moravian Love Feast. Surrounded by the soft glow of the beeswax candles, we sang of the heraldic angels, the shepherds who faithfully watched o'er their flocks by night, and the sweet, holy child in a manger. I still get chills running down my spine as I remember the presence of God in that music.

Coffee and sweet rolls were shared during the service, an expression of the love feast marked within the Moravian Church. After the transcendent majesty and mystery of the music, the gracious offering of hospitality was a particular reminder of the immanence of God in the incarnation.

It is from this tradition that we pray the prayer of the morning star. "Jesus mine, in me shine, Jesus be, constantly, more than thousand suns to me." Jesus said, *"I am the Root and the Offspring of David, and the bright Morning Star"* (Rev. 22:16). As such, the morning star proclaims that the night has ended, that new light has come.

It is no coincidence that within the Moravian tradition, this carol-prayer is a responsive one led by children, just as Isaiah 11 promises, *a little child will lead them* (v. 6). So we pray today the childlike, profound words as the light of the Morning Star shines upon us: "Jesus mine, in me shine."

Prayer Focus: shine in me, Jesus

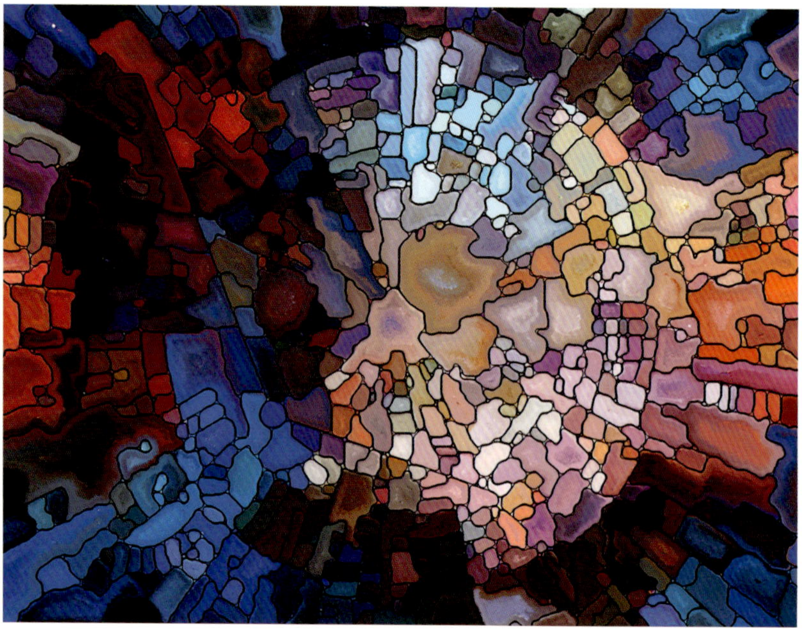

DEC 10

Cradles for the Living Christ

Ralph Spaulding Cushman (20th century)

Let not our hearts be busy inns,
That have no room for Thee,
But cradles for the living Christ and His nativity.
Still driven by a thousand cares
The pilgrims come and go;
The hurried caravans press on;
The inns are crowded so!
Oh, lest we starve, and lest we die in our stupidity,
Come, Holy Child, within and share
Our hospitality.

Because there was no room for them in the inn (Luke 2:7 NIV). A crowded city, all the lodging filled, no room for Jesus. The image, as Cushman points out, speaks to the one who is too busy, whose heart is too crowded to believe.

Yet it speaks as well to the believers, to those who say, "Yes, Lord Jesus, come into my heart," yet find that heart over time crowded with the cares of this world, with the busyness of a life of faith, and yes, with way too many messages in our in-boxes.

I made a feeble attempt at creating a flannelgraph presentation many years ago based on a short story, "My Heart, Christ's Home." The storyteller invited Christ into his home (his heart), and moved from room to room as they explored together what the life of faith meant in the experience of the everyday.

At one point, Jesus tells the narrator that he'd been waiting for him every morning in the (with)drawing room, but that he'd been lonely, as the narrator didn't appear. To paraphrase, Jesus reminded the young man that their time together mattered to Jesus just as much as it mattered to him. Makes me wonder, how often has Jesus been sitting alone, waiting for me to join him?

Prayer Focus: room for Jesus

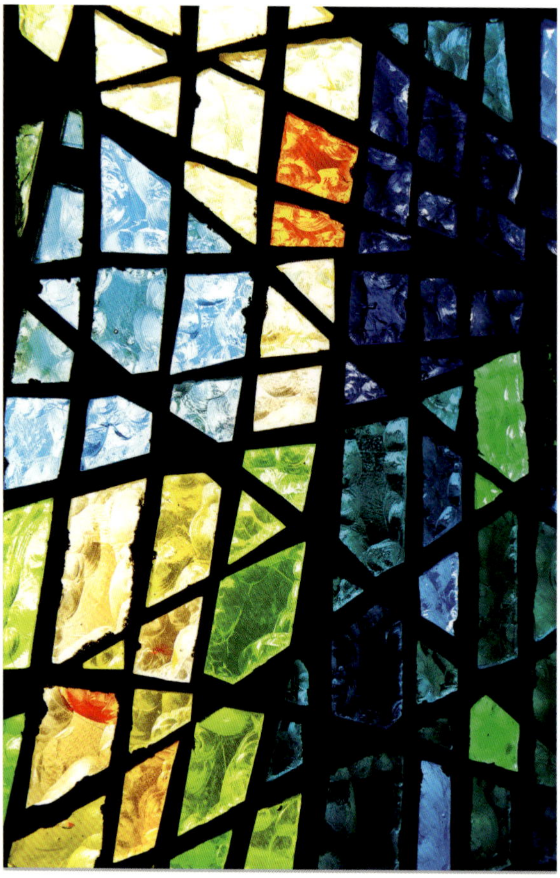

DEC 11

Prayer for the Feast of Christmas
Traditional Orthodox Prayer

Before Thy birth, O Lord, the angelic hosts looked with trembling on this mystery and were struck with wonder: for Thou who hast adorned the vault of heaven with stars hast been well pleased to be born as a babe; and Thou who holdest all the ends of the earth in the hollow of Thy hand art laid in a manger of dumb beasts.
For by such a dispensation has Thy compassion been made known, O Christ, and Thy great mercy: glory to Thee.
Today Christ is born of the Virgin in Bethlehem.
Today He who knows no beginning now begins to be, and the Word is made flesh.
The powers of heaven greatly rejoice and the earth with mankind makes glad.
The Magi offer gifts, the shepherd proclaim the marvel, and we cry aloud without ceasing: Glory to God in the highest, and on earth peace, good will among men.

"The angelic hosts looked with trembling." When was the last time we came with "trembling" to a worship service or dropped to our knees, "sore afraid" in the presence of the Almighty God? In the attempt of the church to make its experience seeker-friendly and its message palatable to the listener, has the sense of awe disappeared? As the stories of the gospels are told through the lips of Larry the Cucumber and Bob the Tomato, do our children lose the sense of mystery, that the word is truly made flesh?

Yes, as the spiritual mournfully tells us, "O, sometimes it causes me to tremble, tremble, tremble." Not just the death and resurrection of Jesus, but his reconciling birth as well. "Glory to God in the highest!"

Prayer Focus: to worship with awe and trembling

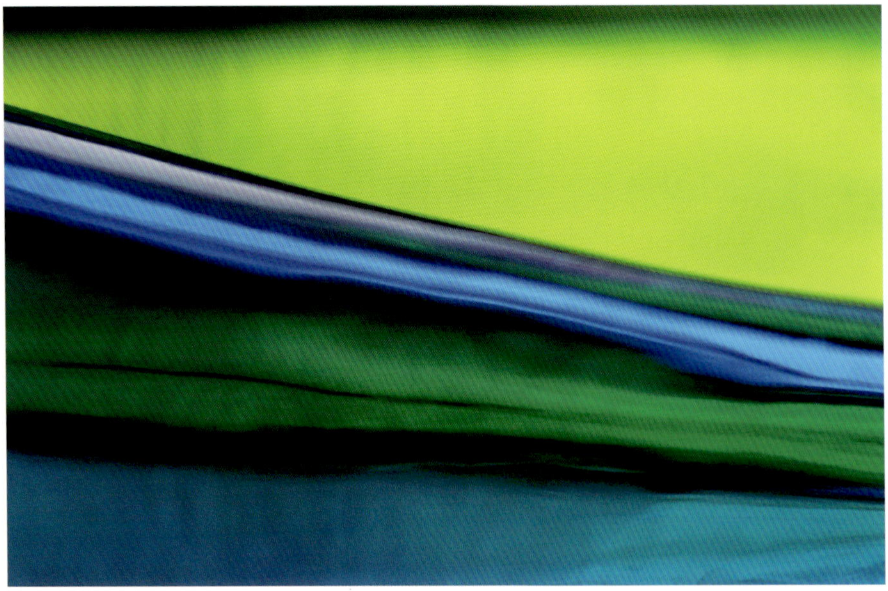

DEC 12

Advent Evening Hymn
8th Century

Come, Sun and Savior, to embrace
Our gloomy world, its weary race,
As groom to bride, as bride to groom:
The wedding chamber, Mary's womb.
At your great Name, O Jesus, now
All knees must bend, all hearts must bow;
All things on earth with one accord,
Like those in heaven, shall call you Lord.
Come in your holy might, we pray,
Redeem us for eternal day;
Defend us while we dwell below,
From all assaults of our dread foe.

This eighth century prayer introduces an image that is rarely seen in Advent and Christmas writings and prayers: that of Mary's womb being the bridal chamber. As noted in the Gospels, Christ is to be the bridegroom (Matthew 9), so it truly is in Mary's womb that his identity begins to develop.

The imagery is inviting, both as Matthew describes for us and as used in the conclusion of the book of Revelation, as the Lamb awaits his bride, the church. *Let us rejoice and be glad and give him glory! For the wedding of the Lamb has come, and his bride has made herself ready* (Rev. 19:7). *Fine linen, bright and clean—that's what the bride is wearing, the righteous acts of God's people* (Rev. 19:8).

Truly, we who love Jesus long to be his bride, to stand before him forgiven, cleansed, pure. Not the bride of a baby in the womb, but the bride of the Lamb. Hallelujah!

Prayer Focus: to be the bride of Christ

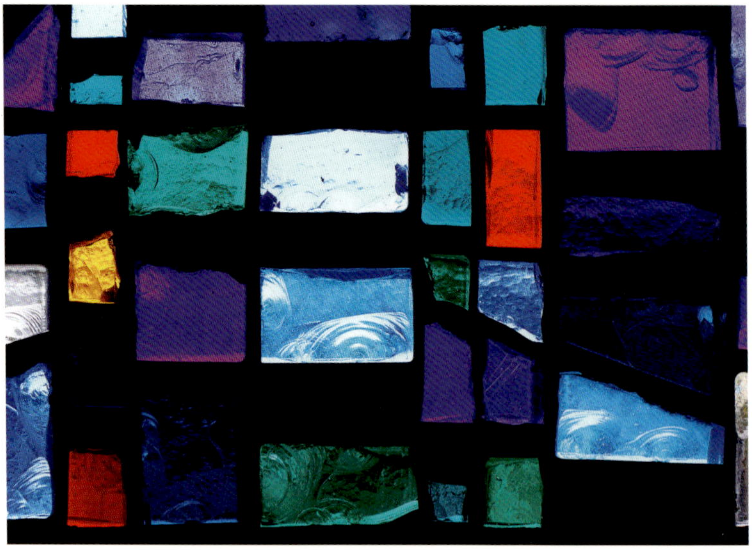

DEC 13

Christmas Prayer

W.E.B. DuBois (1910)

O Thou Incarnate Word of God to man,
make us this Christmas night to realize Thy truth:
we are not Christian because we possess Thy name and celebrate the
ceremonies and idly reiterate the prayers of the church,
but only in so far as we really comprehend and follow the Christ spirit—
we must be poor and not rich,
meek and not proud,
merciful and not oppressors,
peaceful and not warlike or quarrelsome.
For the sake of the righteousness of our cause we must bow to persecution
and reviling, and again and again turn the stricken cheek to the striker,
and above all the cause of our neighbor must be dearer to us,
dearer than our own cause.
This is Christianity. God help us all to be Christians. Amen.

W.E.B. DuBois was active in civil rights work in the first half of the twentieth century, and in that light, his prayer speaks to the life we are called to live as followers of Jesus. His thoughts foreshadow the work of Martin Luther King Jr. and many others, as they urged the spirit of non-violence upon those intent on pursuing societal change.

These are all scriptural images—that of poverty, of meekness, of mercy and of peace. We know we are called to bow to persecution, and to turn the stricken cheek, but this is not an easy road. To be abused, to suffer, to sacrifice—those are not twenty-first century norms.

Yet DuBois gives us hope: "God help us all to be Christians." Christianity is not a lifestyle or a pattern of behaviors that we achieve through pure willpower or effort. It is the Christ spirit in us. We are no longer our own. We are his.

Prayer Focus: a surrendered spirit

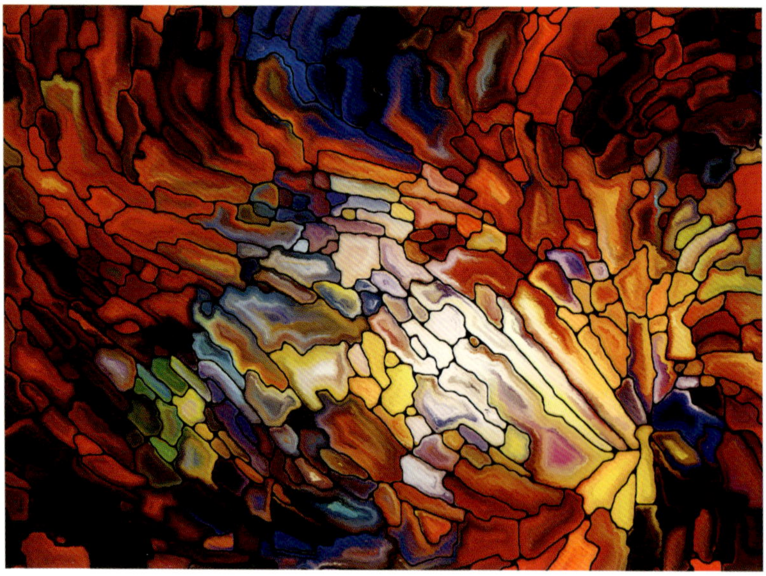

DEC 14

O Little Town of Bethlehem

Philip Brooks (1867)

O holy Child of Bethlehem,
Descend to us, we pray;
Cast out our sin, and enter in,
Be born in us today.
We hear the Christmas angels
The great glad tidings tell;
O come to us, abide with us,
Our Lord Emmanuel!

It is often in the songs of our faith that our corporate prayers are most fully lifted to heaven. In this familiar carol, Brooks uses simple phrases to speak to the desire of our hearts: descend to us, cast out our sin, enter in, be born in us, come to us, abide with us.

What strikes me in these words is that this is what God is already doing, has already done, in the birth and the resurrection. Jesus descended—*he made himself nothing* (Phil. 2:7). He came to take away the sins of the world (John 1:29). He became Emmanuel, God with us (Matt. 1:23). He is born in us (John 3:16). He has come to us (John 1:14), and he promises to abide with us (John 15).

Yet these words remain prayers of petition, of invitation in the present. Even as all of these actions were completed through the incarnation of Christ, they remain a welcome to be extended, a choice to be made day by day in the lives of seekers, of followers, of the faithful. Descend, cast out, enter, be born, come, abide.

In the seldom-used fourth verse of Brooks' original carol, he reminds us of the approach to these prayers: "faith holds wide the door." O holy Child of Bethlehem, this we pray, in faith believing. Amen.

Prayer Focus: open doors

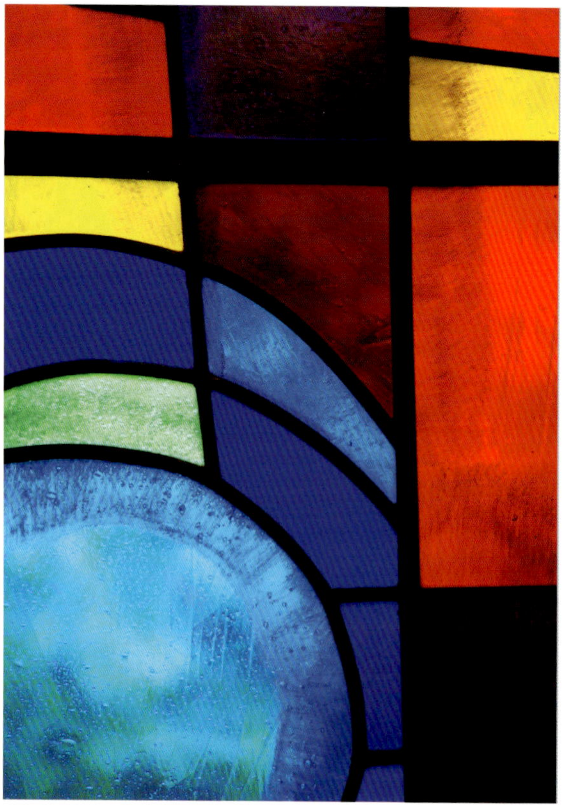

DEC 15

In the Bleak Midwinter

Christina G. Rossetti (19th century)

What can I give him,
Poor as I am?
If I were a shepherd,
I would bring a lamb;
If I were a wise man,
I would do my part;
Yet what I can I give him —
Give my heart.

Often used as a stand-alone quotation, Rossetti's "What can I give him" verse was the fifth stanza of the poem and carol, "In the Bleak Midwinter." Her simple question continues to be one of significance: What can I give him? From the perspective of the one with no lamb and none of the riches of the Magi, empty hands seem unable to bring a gift of value to the Savior.

Yet even for those of us who are able to bring a material item of value to the manger of the Christ child, Rossetti's answer becomes the one of most value—"Give my heart." Because in the end, what can we truly give to Christ? After all, all that we have comes to us from God.

As Frances Havergal suggests in her beloved hymn, we can give (offer to God for the taking) our moments, our days, our hands, our feet, our voices, our lips, our silver and gold, and our intellect. Yet she too concludes with Rossetti, it is the self that remains ours to give, and that becomes the most precious, the most profound gift to the Christ.

Take my will, and make it Thine; it shall be no longer mine.
Take my heart, it is Thine own; it shall be Thy royal throne.
Take my love, my Lord, I pour at Thy feet its treasure store.
Take myself, and I will be ever, only, all for Thee.

Prayer Focus: take my life

WE HEAR THE ANGELS | 33

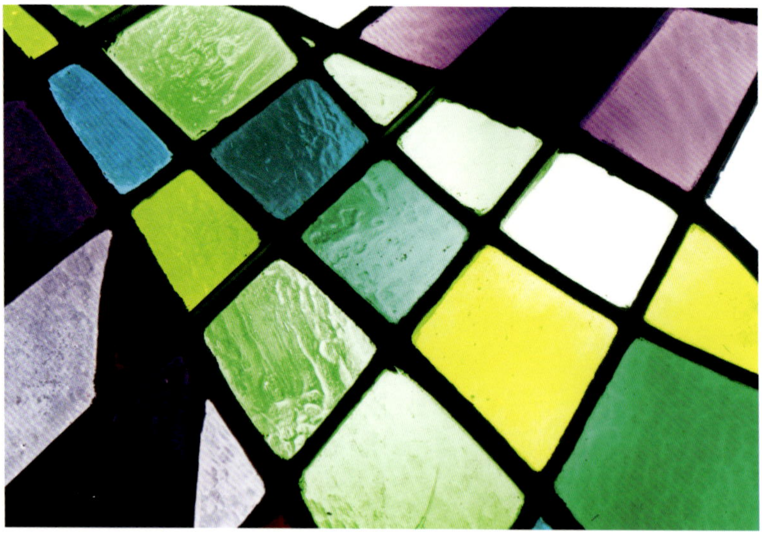

DEC 16

Father, Our Hearts We Lift

Charles Wesley (18th century)

Father, our hearts we lift
Up to Thy gracious throne,
And bless Thee for the precious gift
Of Thine incarnate Son;
The Gift unspeakable
We thankfully receive,
And to the world Thy goodness tell,
And to Thy glory live.

Charles Wesley, writer of more than 6000 hymns, is best known at Christmas for "Hark, the Herald Angels Sing." Yet in this carol-prayer, Wesley prays of the gratitude that comes as a result of the unspeakable gift of God to us, his people.

While twenty-first century marketing gurus want us to believe that the greatest gift we receive at Christmas is the one with the biggest price tag (a diamond ring, a widescreen TV, a new car), what I've recognized over the years is that it is the gift that comes from the heart, the gift that is a sacrificial one from the giver, that I value most. Those are the gifts that leave me speechless.

Unspeakable, indescribable, inexpressible, too wonderful for words—that's how the various translators describe the gift of God in 2 Corinthians 9:15. In that chapter, Paul has been pointing out the effects of generosity, both in the heart of the giver and in the kingdom of God. It's possible that this phrase is one that Paul uses to describe the gift of grace, and the gift of God's abundant blessings that allows his followers to be generous.

But, as Wesley claims the phrase, it is also descriptive of the gift of Jesus himself—Jesus, the gift from the heart of God.

The irony for the Christian is that while the immensity of the gift of Christ may leave us speechless in the moment of recognition, it demands that we speak of the immensity of the gift to others.

Prayer Focus: the indescribable gift of Jesus

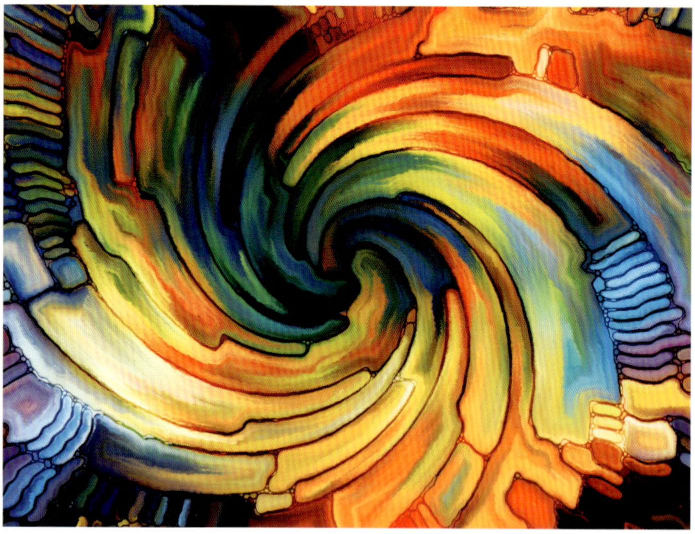

DEC 17

Nativity Prayer of St. Augustine

St. Augustine of Hippo (5th century)

Let the just rejoice,
for their justifier is born.
Let the sick and infirm rejoice,
For their Saviour is born.
Let the captives rejoice,
For their Redeemer is born.
Let slaves rejoice,
for their Master is born.
Let free men rejoice,
For their Liberator is born.
Let All Christians rejoice,
For Jesus Christ is born.

In this ancient prayer, Augustine challenges the pray-ers to rejoice in phrases that connect with their individual places in life. While one human being cannot be all things to all people, Jesus can. Think on these today. Are you standing in righteousness today? It is only because Christ has made you just before the Father. Are you struggling? Your Savior brings you his saving grace. Are you bound in some way, taken captive by desires, addictions, and tenacious habits? There is one who redeems you.

Even for those who are bound in slavery—through abusive marriages, through human trafficking, through economic bondage, or through besetting sin—Jesus stands ready to be your Master. And, as Augustine reminds us, even for the one who sees himself/herself as a free person, it is because of liberation in Christ.

Yes, today is a day of rejoicing. In Christ, God meets us where we are and provides just what we need for the day. That's a hallelujah moment for sure.

Prayer Focus: rejoice!

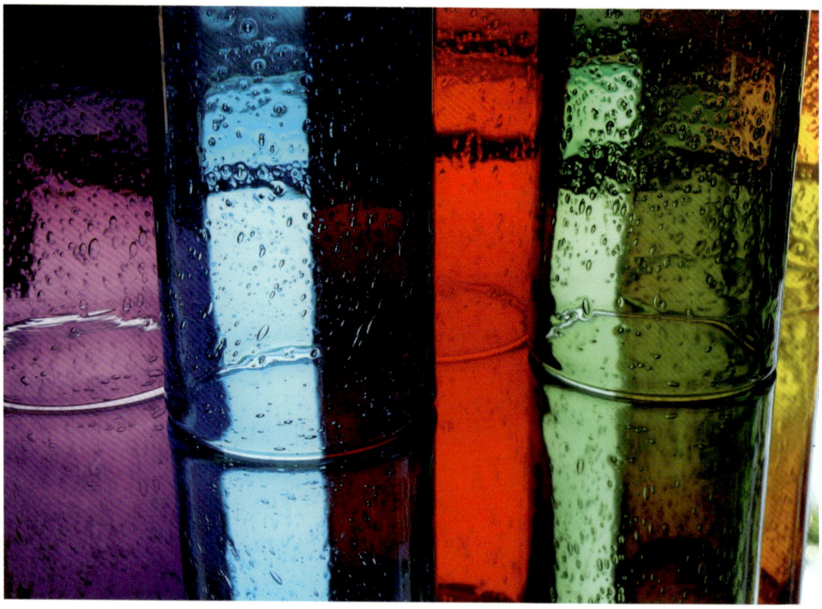

DEC 18

A Clear Light
Hildegard of Bingen (12th century)

The Word made flesh for us gives us the greatest hope
that the murky night of darkness will not overwhelm us,
but we shall see the daylight of eternity.
Lord, let us receive your clear light; be for us such a mirror of light
that we may be given grace to see you unendingly.
If we are overcome, you have the power to forgive us;
Therefore, in my sin I call on you, my Lord, my Light, for help.
For you were sent into the world to enlighten my heart,
to nurture true repentance and to make the Holy Spirit's
work grow more powerfully in me.
With the Father and the Holy Spirit you live and reign forever!

Have you ever been overwhelmed by the murky night of darkness? Gloomy, misty, cloudy, muddy, dim, overshadowed? There is a darkness of night that is glorious, when the sky is clear, the stars are brilliant, and the moon shines as a crescent of light and hope. But then there are the murky nights, when the air is as heavy as our hearts, and clouds cover any hope of illumination.

The incarnation, Hildegard claims, brings a clear, true light that calls us to action—to call upon God in the midst of the murkiness, to look into our hearts with a sense of enlightenment that comes through the Spirit of God, and to nurture true repentance, not just one of confession but one of a turning from sin, a new path, a clean heart. We no longer can be content with the funhouse mirror that distorts our likeness—no, we long for the mirror of light that will allow us to see clearly and respond in faith.

Prayer Focus: enlightened hearts

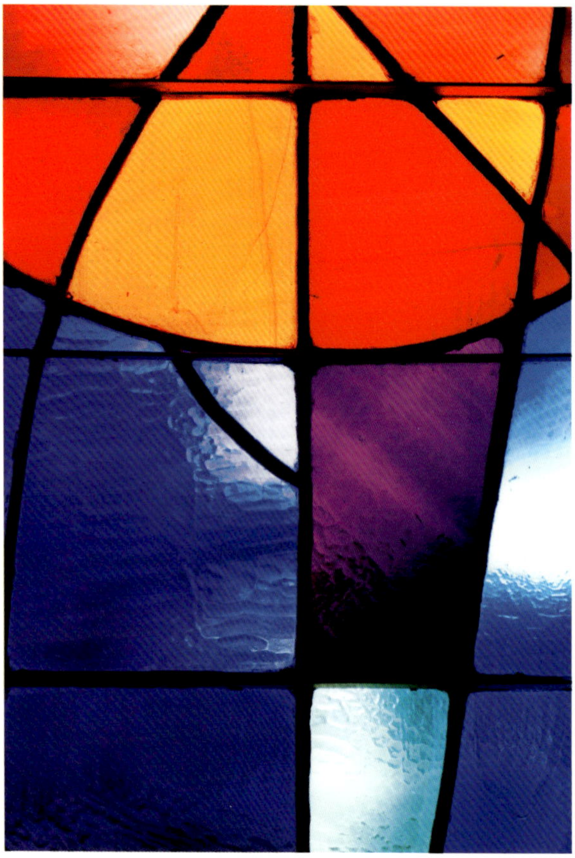

DEC 19

Balulalow

James, John and Robert Wedderbrun (16th century)

O my dear heart, young Jesus sweet,
Prepare thy cradle in my spirit.
And I shall rock thee in my heart
And never more from thee depart.
But I shall praise thee evermore
With songs sweet to thy glory,
The knees of my heart shall I bow,
And sing that right Balulalow.

The Celts speak of liminal space or "thin space," that time/place where God seems especially present, where earth nearly touches heaven. We stumble upon these thin spaces, sometimes in church, sometimes in nature, and sometimes in the rocking chair as we whisper a lullaby to a "precious wee bairn."

It is a "thin space" lullaby that makes up this prayer of the Wedderbrun brothers. Balulalow is Scottish for lullaby, making this prayer/poem a lullaby to the Christ child. I love the intimacy: "I shall rock thee in my heart." The rhythm of the heartbeat, the rhythm of the rocking chair, combine to create a settled sense of time, of presence.

I picture the young mother Mary, rocking her babe as she is propped against a mound of hay in the stable, or cradling her son in the dark of night on the road to Egypt, once more holding the words of Gabriel deep within. It is that image that I cling to, as I open my heart to this babe, this redeemer, this savior.

With Mary I sing, I pray, the knees of my heart bow: Balulalow, Jesus, balualow.

Prayer Focus: every knee shall bow

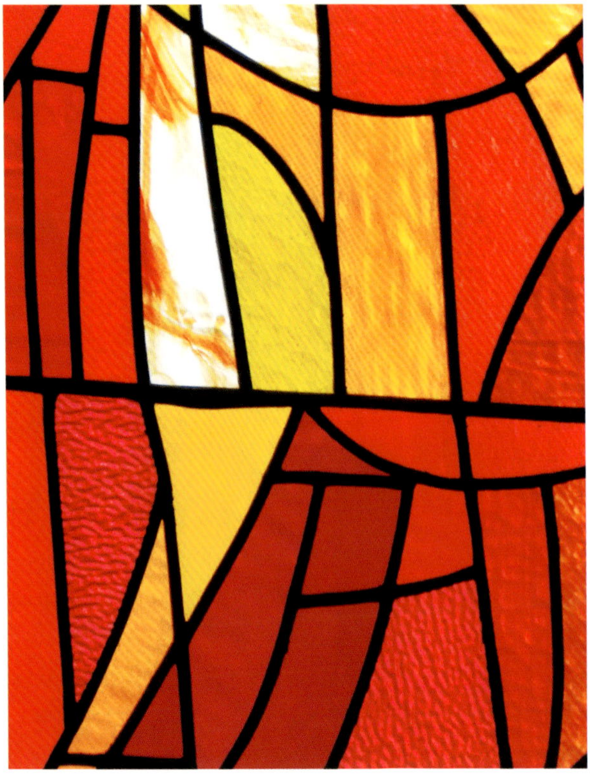

DEC 20

Moonless Darkness Stands Between

Gerard Manley Hopkins (19th century)

Moonless darkness stands between.
Past, the Past, no more be seen!
But the Bethlehem star may lead me
To the sight of Him who freed me
From the self that I have been.
Make me pure, Lord: Thou art holy;
Make me meek, Lord: Thou wert lowly;
Now beginning, and always,
Now begin, on Christmas day.

As Manley suggests in the last line of his prayer, the marking of a holy day such as Christmas can provide the impetus to a new beginning, a beginning in which the past is no more seen. We know that we need not wait for any special day to pray a prayer of repentance, but Christmas can become a time when our hearts are stirred to seek after the purity and holiness of Christ in a way we have not done before.

The danger is that the coming of Christmas will find us far from that awareness, with a hectic pace that tempts us to add one more purchase or one more party to our already overburdened lives. While Hopkins never experienced a twenty-first century lifestyle, his reminder of the role of the Bethlehem star in his own experience of freedom can be ours as well. We can be freed from "the self that I have been," particularly when that self is far from pure, far from meek. 'Would you be free from your burden of sin?" the songwriter asks. There is "power in the blood," power in the One who came in the light of the Bethlehem star.

Prayer Focus: freedom to be Christ's

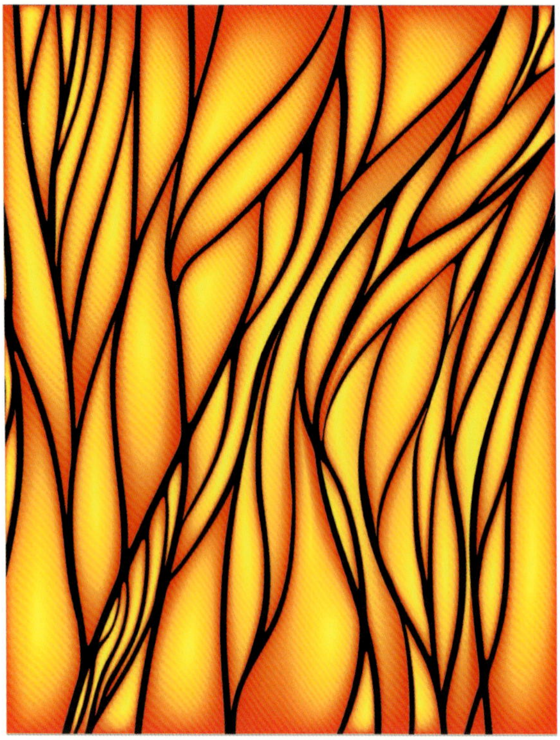

DEC 21

Come, Come, Jesus, I Await You

Angelo Giuseppe Roncalli (20th century)

I am a poor shepherd; I have only a wretched stable,
a small manger, some wisps of straw.
I offer all these to you, be pleased to come into my poor hovel.
I offer you my heart; my soul is poor and bare of virtues,
the straws of so many imperfections will prick you and make you weep—
but oh, my Lord, what can you expect?
This little is all I have. . . .
I have nothing better to offer you, Jesus,
honour my soul with your presence, adorn it with your graces.
Burn this straw and change it into a soft couch
for your most holy body.

This prayer, excerpted from the words of a man who would one day be Pope John XXIII, is a mirror into the soul of the young Angelo Giuseppe Roncalli. "The straws of so many imperfections will prick you and make you weep." Ah, that is a man who is seeking the heart of God, who knows his own heart's failings and the pain those imperfections will bring to God.

The image is powerful—we've felt the pricks and stabs of the straw on a hayride, and cringe at the thought of a baby pillowed in a bed of straw—especially the straw of our own making.

It is an encouragement to our hearts that the offerings of that poor shepherd, the fourth-born child of a sharecropper with his wisps of straw, were so adorned with the grace of God that he became a beloved pope as well as a courageous leader.

So it can be for us as well, when we name the straw that brings tears to the eyes of Jesus, and then bring that straw in repentance, offering what little we have to God.

Prayer Focus: our wisps of straw

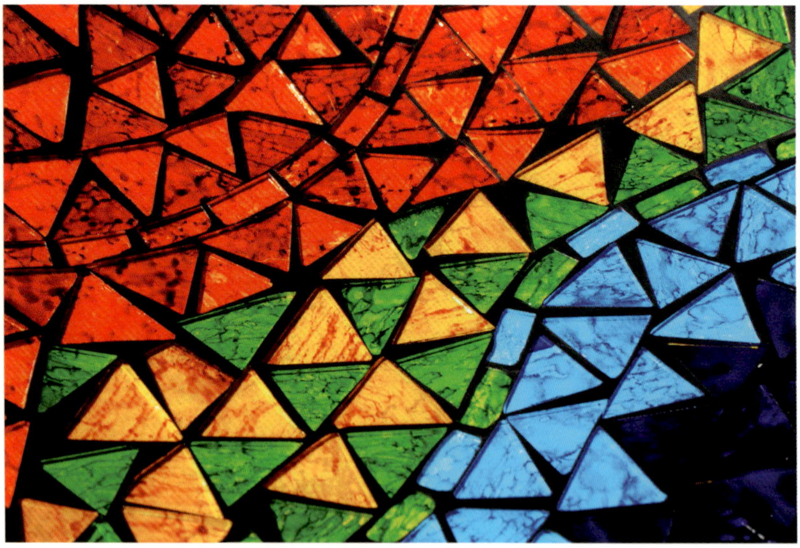

A Christmas Prayer

Robert Louis Stevenson (19th century)

Loving God, Help us remember the birth of Jesus,
that we may share in the song of the angels,
the gladness of the shepherds,
and worship of the wise men.
Close the door of hate
and open the door of love all over the world.
Let kindness come with every gift and
good desires with every greeting.
Deliver us from evil by the blessing which Christ brings,
and teach us to be merry with clear hearts.
May the Christmas morning make us happy to be thy children,
and Christmas evening bring us to our beds with grateful thoughts,
forgiving and forgiven, for Jesus' sake. Amen.

Stevenson's prayer is one worth repeating. What a privilege to share in the song of the angels, to be able to shout, "Glory to God in the highest." How exciting to experience the thrill of the shepherds as they ran to the stable and discovered the baby Jesus. How we long to worship at the manger of Christ as did the wise men, offering our gifts to him.

Yes, Christmas is a time of rejoicing, and we long to be part of the sacred response of the ages, with love from that stable pouring out into the world. That's the joyous hope as we celebrate Christmas year after year.

Yet we cannot leave this prayer without noting the last phrase, so striking in its description of the one who is praying: forgiving and forgiven. Yes, kindness, good desires, merry hearts and grateful thoughts are good gifts to be received. But without the forgiveness that comes through the incarnation, and the forgiving that we offer one to another on a daily basis, we are missing the redemptive reason for the birth.

Prayer Focus: forgiveness

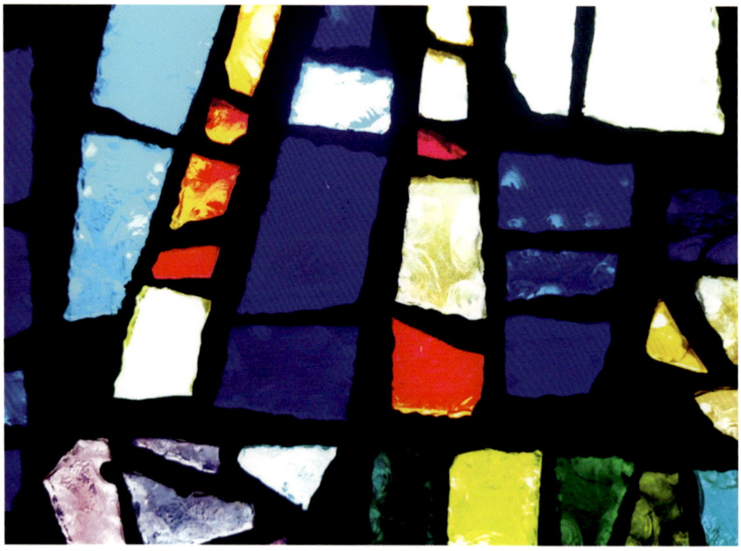

DEC 23

Come to My Heart

Emily E. Elliot (1864)

Thou didst leave thy throne and thy kingly crown,
When thou camest to earth for me,
But in Bethlehem's home there was found no room,
For thy holy nativity.
O Come to my heart, Lord Jesus,
There is room in my heart for thee.

The theme is a common one in literature, fairy tales and film—the prince lives in the guise of a pauper, or the child born to royalty is hidden among commoners or under a spell. In the twenty-first century kids' film genre, there is even a Barbie movie where the princess and the popstar change places. In the movies it's a fun experiment, but the stakes were tremendously higher in the sacred drama of the incarnation.

The willingness to exchange the throne of heaven for a life of rejection and sorrow on earth is the hard-to-believe part of the gospel from a human perspective. Why would the Almighty God of the universe send his son to a time and place where he wouldn't be received as deity? As written in the gospel of John, *He was in the world, and though the world was made through him, the world did not recognize him. He came to that which was his own, but his own did not receive him* (John 1:10-11).

From our human view, we can't understand why this would have to be. Why was there no room in the inn? Why was the son of God despised and rejected? No, we can't fathom why God would choose this for his only son. We can only accept with gratitude the gift that it was—and is—to us. Because, as John continues to tell us, *Yet to all who did receive him, to those who believed in his name, he gave the right to become children of God* (John 1:12). That is the wonder, the amazing grace of the incarnation.

Prayer Focus: the incarnation

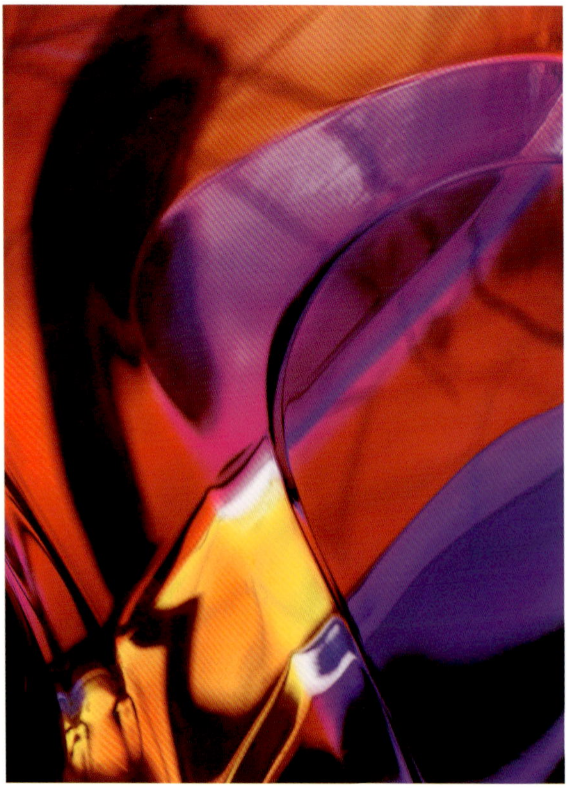

DEC 24

Christmas Eve Prayer
Frank Borman, Apollo 8 space mission, 1968

Give us, O God, the vision which can see Your love in the world
in spite of human failure.
Give us the faith to trust Your goodness
in spite of our ignorance and weakness.
Give us the knowledge that we may continue to pray
with understanding hearts.
And show us what each one of us can do
to set forward the coming of the day of universal peace.

Knowing that he would be circling the moon on Christmas Eve, Bornam and his friend Rod Rose chose the above prayer to be shared from outer space on December 24, 1968. His prayerful focus on the failure, ignorance and weakness of humans is in sharp contrast to the power and success that the space program symbolized.

As an astronaut, it would have been understandable for Borman to worship the gods of science and of accomplishment that took him to the moon, but instead he draws us back to the God of the universe, a God of love and goodness. It is in this God's name that he prays for the universal peace that has so eluded the world.

It is this call to peace that echoes the words spoken the first Christmas—peace on earth. Jill and Sy Miller conclude their popular song with the phrase "Let there be peace on earth and let it begin with me," and Borman asks for God's guidance for that same task—"show us what each one of us can do." Whether orbiting the moon or going about my daily business, show me, O God, what I can do to live a life of peace and to bring peace to my small corner of the world.

Prayer Focus: peace on earth

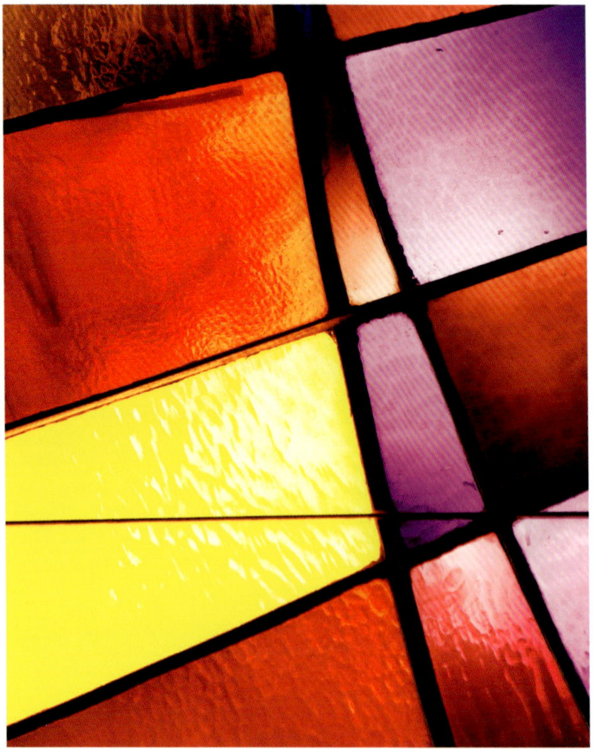

DEC 25

Christmas Dinner Prayer

Martin Luther (16th century)

Ah, dearest Jesus, holy Child,
Make thee a bed, soft, undefiled,
Within my heart, that it may be
A quiet chamber kept for Thee.

My heart for very joy doth leap,
My lips no more can silence keep,
I too must sing, with joyful tongue,
That sweetest ancient song,

Glory to God in highest heaven,
Who unto man His Son hath given
While angels sing with pious mirth.
A glad new year to all the earth!

    This Christmas dinner prayer concludes our journey through the days leading up to Christmas with a prayer of joy. While we may picture the angelic visitors to the shepherds as being full of joy, the phrase "pious mirth" seems at first glance to be a juxtaposition of words. While I recognize that pious means devout or sacred, I would also think of a straight-laced, sour-faced saint as an example of piety.

    But here Luther connects "pious" with "mirth," adding laughter, hilarity, glee and joy to the description of the angels' song. How perfect for Christmas. Overshadowed as we know it to be by the cross, for one moment in time, the sacred is filled with joy, the devout are given permission to laugh and dance and be full of joy.

    That's the gift of Christmas for us. Our heart "for very joy doth leap" because of the coming of Jesus to the world. It is a day for merrymaking, for laughter, for delight and for joy. Glory to God in the highest!

Prayer Focus: joy

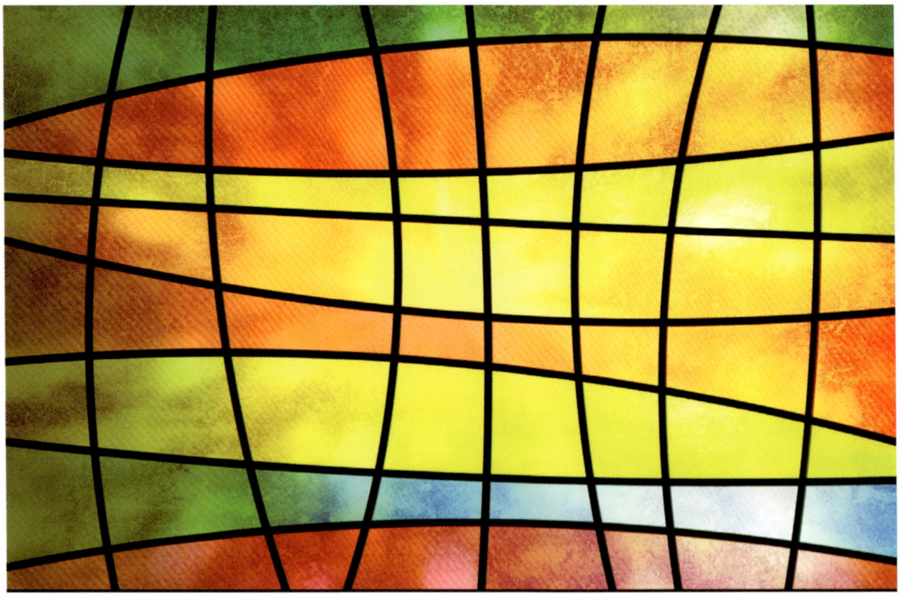

The Great "O" Antiphons—Seven brief prayers traditionally chanted or sung
at evening worship services during Advent.

O Wisdom, O holy word of God,
You govern all creation with your strong, yet tender care.
Come, and show your people the way to salvation.

O Sacred Lord of ancient Israel,
Who showed yourself to Moses in the burning bush,
Who gave him the holy law on Sinai mountain;
Come, stretch out your mighty hand to set us free.

O Flower of Jesse's stem,
You have been raised up as a sign for all peoples;
Kings stand silent in your presence;
The nations bow down in worship before you.
Come, let nothing keep you from coming to our aid.

O Key of David, O Royal Power of Israel,
Controlling at your will the gate of heaven;
Come, break down the prison walls of death
For those who dwell in darkness and the shadow of death;
And lead your captive people into freedom.

O Radiant Dawn, splendor of eternal light,
Sun of Justice,
Come shine on those who dwell in darkness
and the shadow of death.

O King of all the nations
The only joy of every human heart;
O Keystone of the mighty arch of man,
Come and save the creature you fashioned from the dust.

O Emmanuel, King and Lawgiver, Desire of the nations,
Savior of all people,
Come and set us free, Lord, our God.